VIOLIN REPERTOIRE ALBUM 1

VIOLIN SERIES

1

ISBN 0-88797-355-8

Official Examination Repertoire of
THE ROYAL CONSERVATORY OF MUSIC
Grade 1

FREDERICK
HARRIS
MUSIC

Répertoire officiel des examens
THE ROYAL CONSERVATORY OF MUSIC
Niveau 1

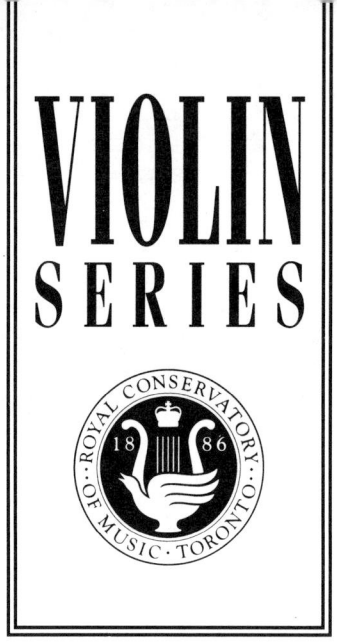

*T*he *Violin Series* of The Royal Conservatory of Music includes a body of essential repertoire and technique that has been carefully selected and edited to benefit students, teachers, and those who play the violin solely for their own enjoyment. In addition to standard repertoire, this *Violin Series* contains new arrangements, editions, and works composed especially for the collection. Careful attention has been given to the authority of the editions and to the pedagogical and academic integrity of the editing.

The primary goal of this series is to support the artistic and technical development of violinists learning their craft. Part of that craft involves a subtle understanding of the relationship between expression, style, and technique. It should be noted that fingerings and bowings printed in the series are suggestions only and are not mandatory. Students are encouraged, however, to use fingerings and bowings which reflect current technical study.

A secure musical development depends upon organized and patient study. This collection affords the student the opportunity to experience a broad variety of styles and techniques.

The repertoire and technique in this *Violin Series* are drawn from The Royal Conservatory of Music Violin Syllabus. In preparing for Royal Conservatory examinations, students and teachers must consult the current Violin Syllabus for examination procedures and regulations.

*L*e "Violin Series" du Royal Conservatory of Music inclut un corpus de répertoire et d'études techniques recueillis et redigés pour bénéficier les étudiant(e)s et les professeur(e)s, et pour aider ceux et celles qui jouent du violon simplement pour leur intérêt personnel. Cette série contient non seulement des morceaux du répertoire standard, mais aussi de nouveaux arrangements et de nouvelles éditions ainsi que des oeuvres composées spécialement pour la série. L'autorité des éditions et l'intégrité pédagogique et académique des rédactions ont reçu une attention soignée.

Le premier objectif de cette série est celui d'appuyer la formation artistique et technique des violonistes. Une partie intégrante de cette formation implique une compréhension subtile de la relation entre l'expression, le style et la technique. Notez bien que les doigtés et les coups d'archet indiqués ne sont que des suggestions et ne sont pas obligatoires. Néanmoins, nous encourageons les élèves à se servir des doigtés et des coups d'archet qui correspondent à leur niveau technique actuel.

Un développement musical stable et continu dépend d'une étude organisée et patiente. Ce recueil offre à l'étudiant(e) l'occasion d'explorer une grande variété de styles et de techniques.

Le répertoire et la technique de cette "Violin Series" sont puisés au syllabus pour violon du Royal Conservatory of Music. En se préparant pour des examens du conservatoire, les étudiant(e)s et les professeur(e)s doivent consulter les procédures et les réglements du syllabus pour violon de l'année en cours.

THE ROYAL CONSERVATORY OF MUSIC
273 Bloor Street West, Toronto, Ontario, M5S 1W2

Violin Repertoire Album 1
TABLE OF CONTENTS

List A

List B

* Canadian Composer / Compositeur canadien

The repertoire is divided into *List A* and *List B* for the convenience of users of The Royal Conservatory of Music Violin Syllabus. / Le répertoire a été réparti entre "List A" et "List B" pour faciliter votre utilisation du syllabus pour violon du Royal Conservatory of Music.

ANDANTE

LIST A

JOSEPH HAYDN
1732-1809

* Suggested bowing: on the string, middle or upper half. / Coup d'archet suggéré: sur la corde, à mi-corde ou sur la partie supérieure.

Source: Symphony no. 94, "The Surprise" (1791)

Arrangement © copyright 1992 The Frederick Harris Music Co., Limited.

T.V. THEME / THÈME DE TÉLÉ

LIST A

RICKY HYSLOP
b./n. 1915

SWEET BETSY FROM PIKE

TRADITIONAL AMERICAN /
AIR TRADITIONNEL AMÉRICAIN
arranged by / arrangé de Warren Mould
b./n. 1933

LIST A

ANDANTE

LIST A

FRIEDRICH KUHLAU
1786-1832

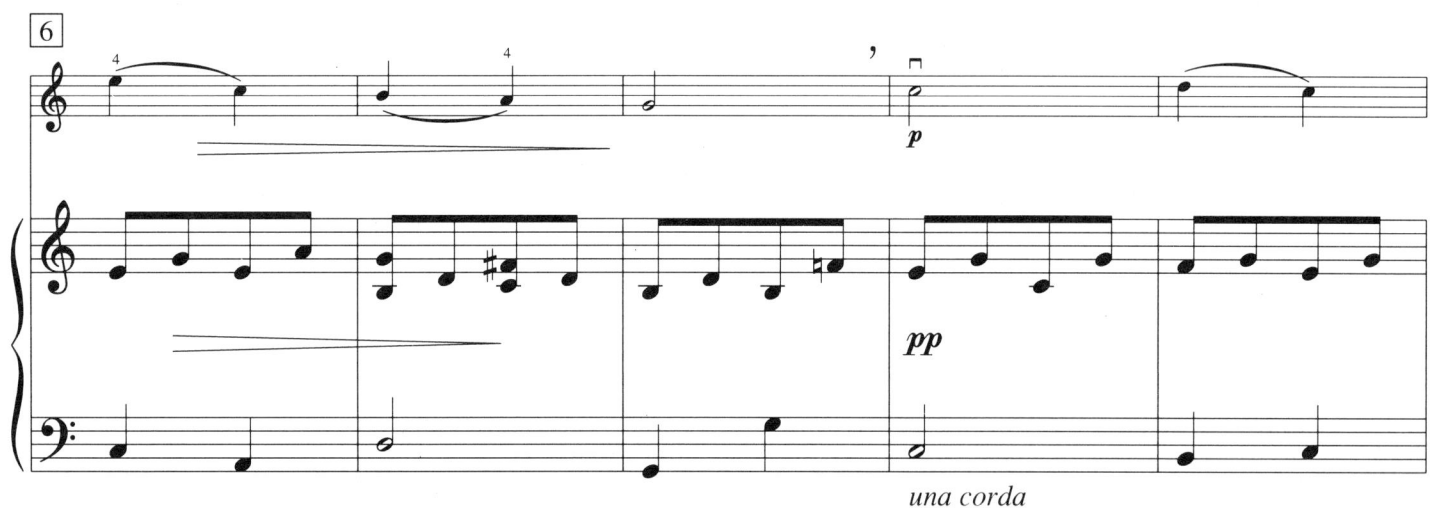

THE SAILBOAT ON THE LAKE / LE VOILIER SUR LE LAC

LIST A

JEAN COULTHARD
b./n. 1908

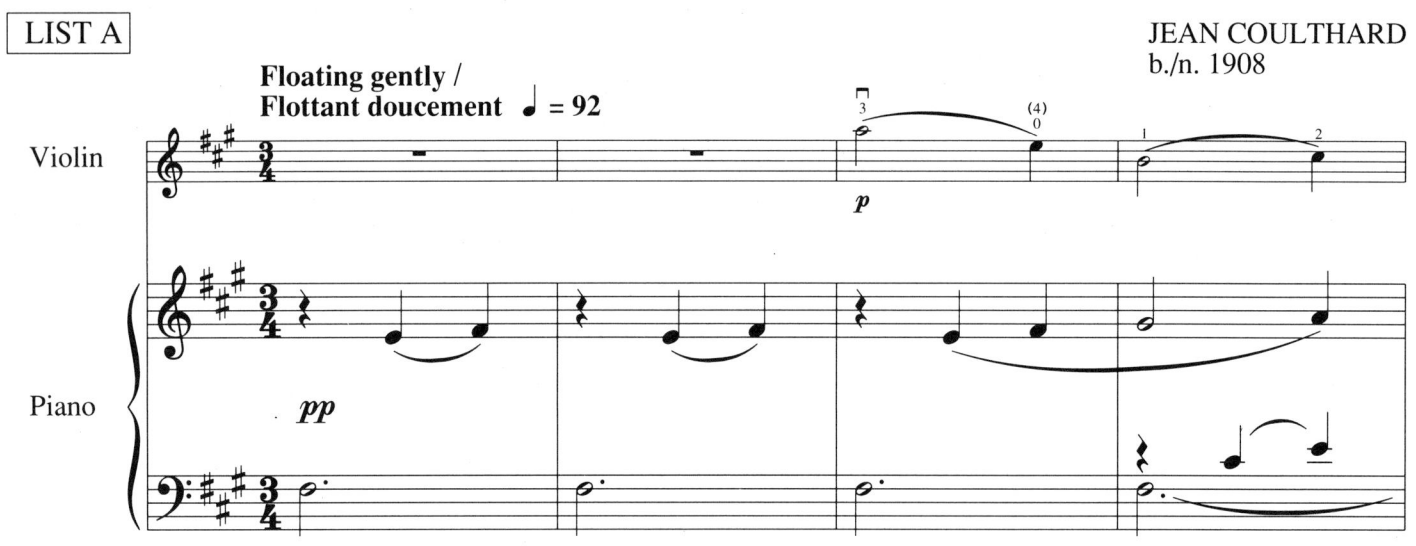

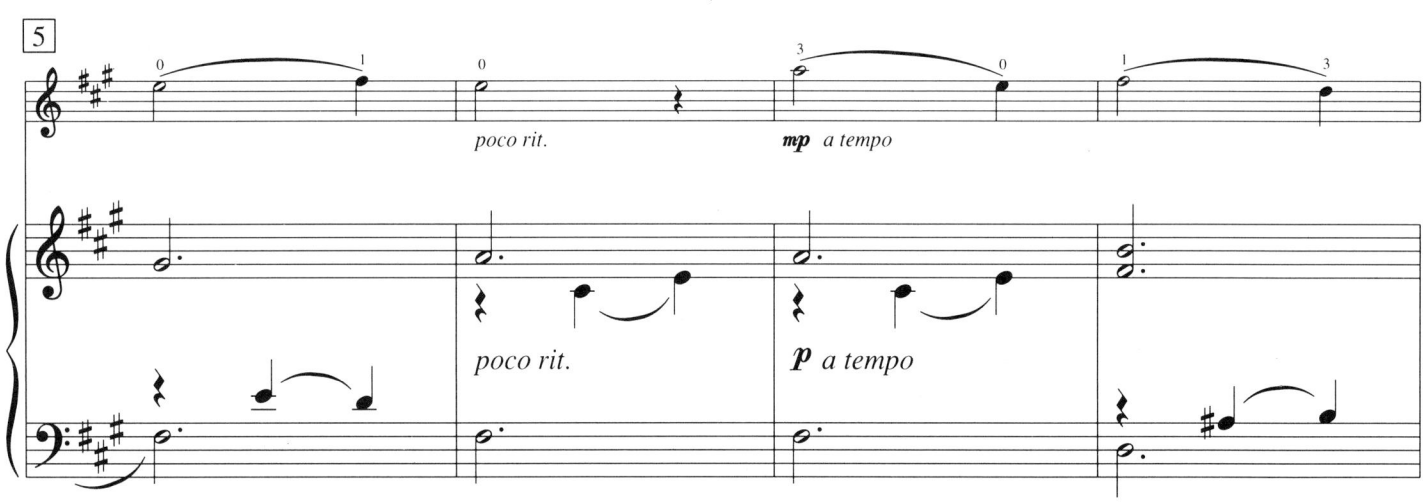

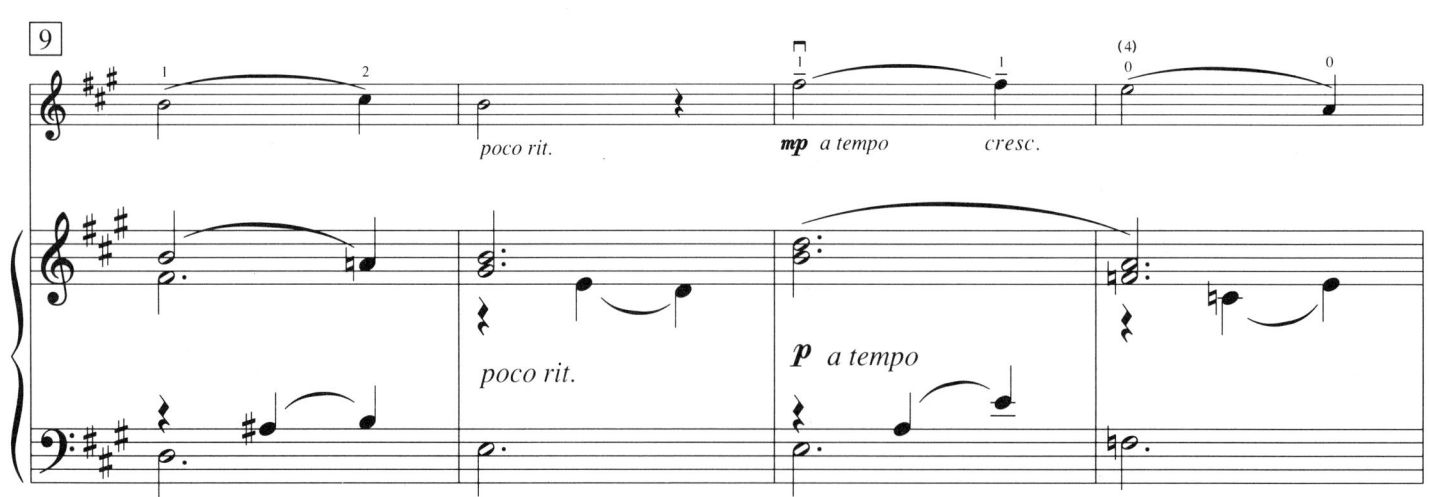

Source: À la Jeunesse, Book 2

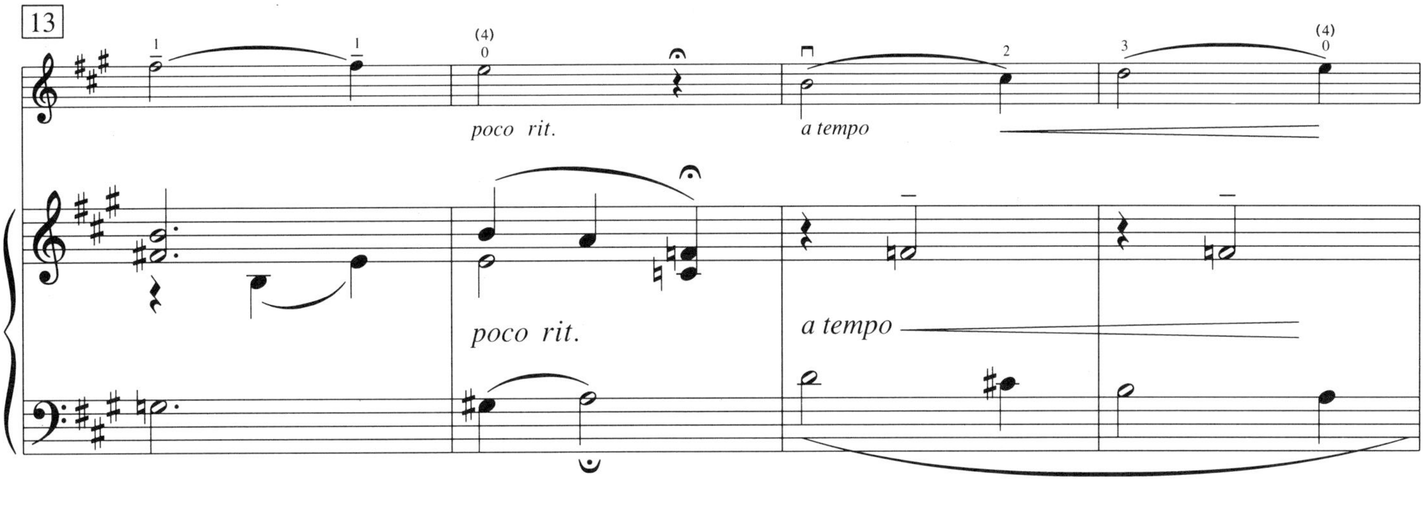

MINUET / MENUET

LIST A

CHRISTOPH WILLIBALD GLUCK
1714-1787

Violin

Piano

Andante grazioso

mp

Source: *"Que d'attraits,"* chorus from Act 1 of *Iphigénie en Aulide* (1744)
Arrangement © copyright 1992 The Frederick Harris Music Co., Limited.

EVENING SONG / CHANSON DU SOIR

LIST A

GEORG C. SCHEMELLI
c. 1676-1762

The introduction is editorial. Use the enharmonic fingering indicated in measure 12. / L'introduction est de la part des rédacteurs. Utiliser le doigté enharmonique tel qu'est indiqué à la mesure 12.

Source: Schemelli's *Musicalisches Gesang-Buch,* no. 39 (1736), for which J.S. Bach supplied the figured bass. / *Musicalisches Gesang-Buch,* nº 39 (1736), de Schemelli, pour lequel J.S. Bach fournit la basse chiffrée.

ON TIP-TOE / SUR LA POINTE DES PIEDS

LIST A

VIOLET ARCHER
b./n. 1913

Source: *Twelve Miniatures*

GRADE 1 - VIOLIN PART

ANDANTE

LIST A

JOSEPH HAYDN
1732-1809

* Suggested bowing: on the string, middle or upper half. / Coup d'archet suggéré: sur la corde, à mi-corde ou sur la partie supérieure.
Source: Symphony no. 94, "The Surprise" (1791)
Arrangement © copyright 1992 The Frederick Harris Music Co., Limited.

T.V. THEME / THÈME DE TÉLÉ

LIST A

RICKY HYSLOP
b./n. 1915

Smoothly gliding / D'un mouvement bien lié ♩ = *c.* 92

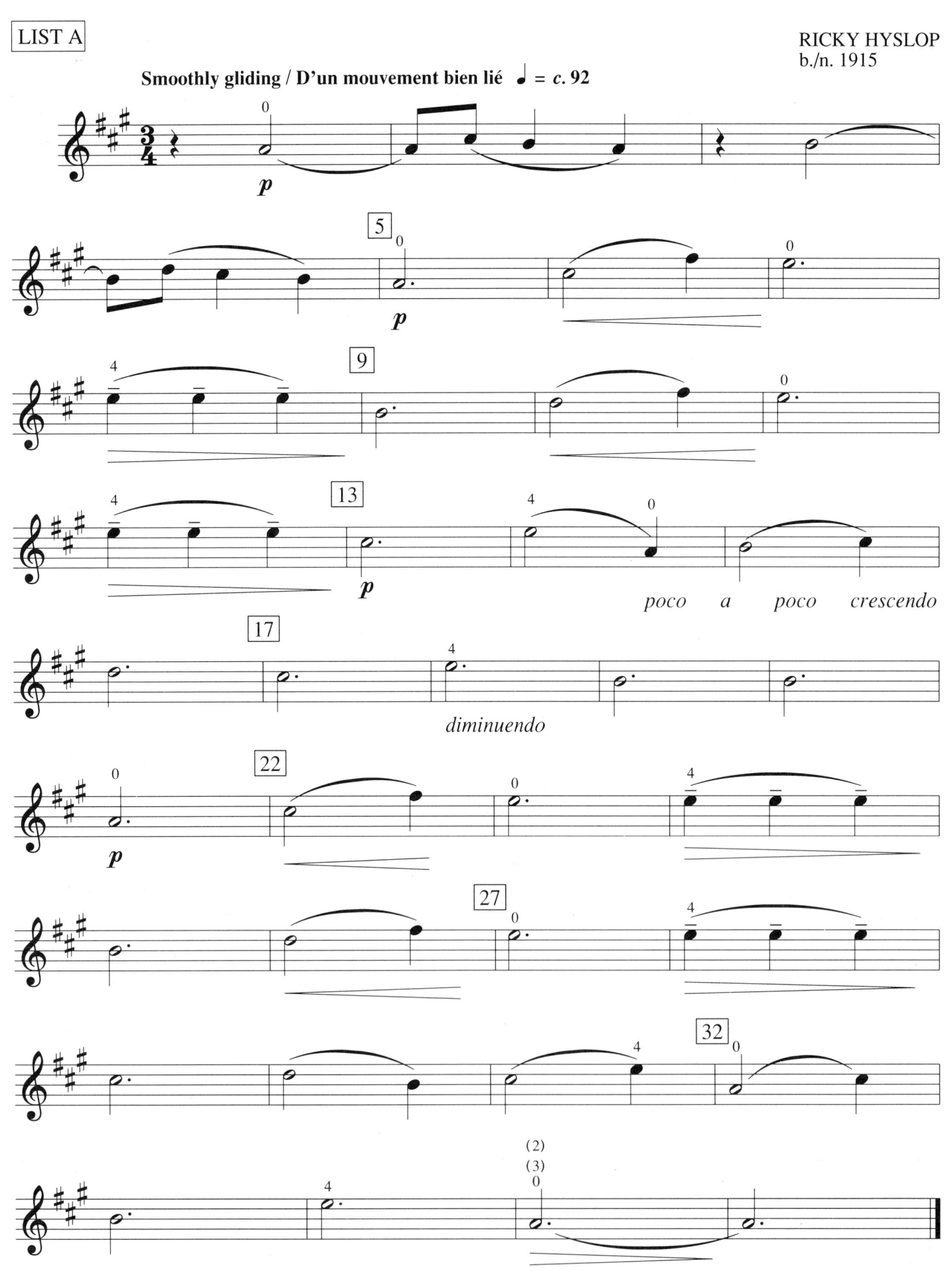

Source: *Music Stands: Easy Solos for Violin*
© Copyright 1987 The Frederick Harris Music Co., Limited.

SWEET BETSY FROM PIKE

TRADITIONAL AMERICAN /
AIR TRADITIONNEL AMÉRICAIN
arranged by / arrangé de Warren Mould
b./n. 1933

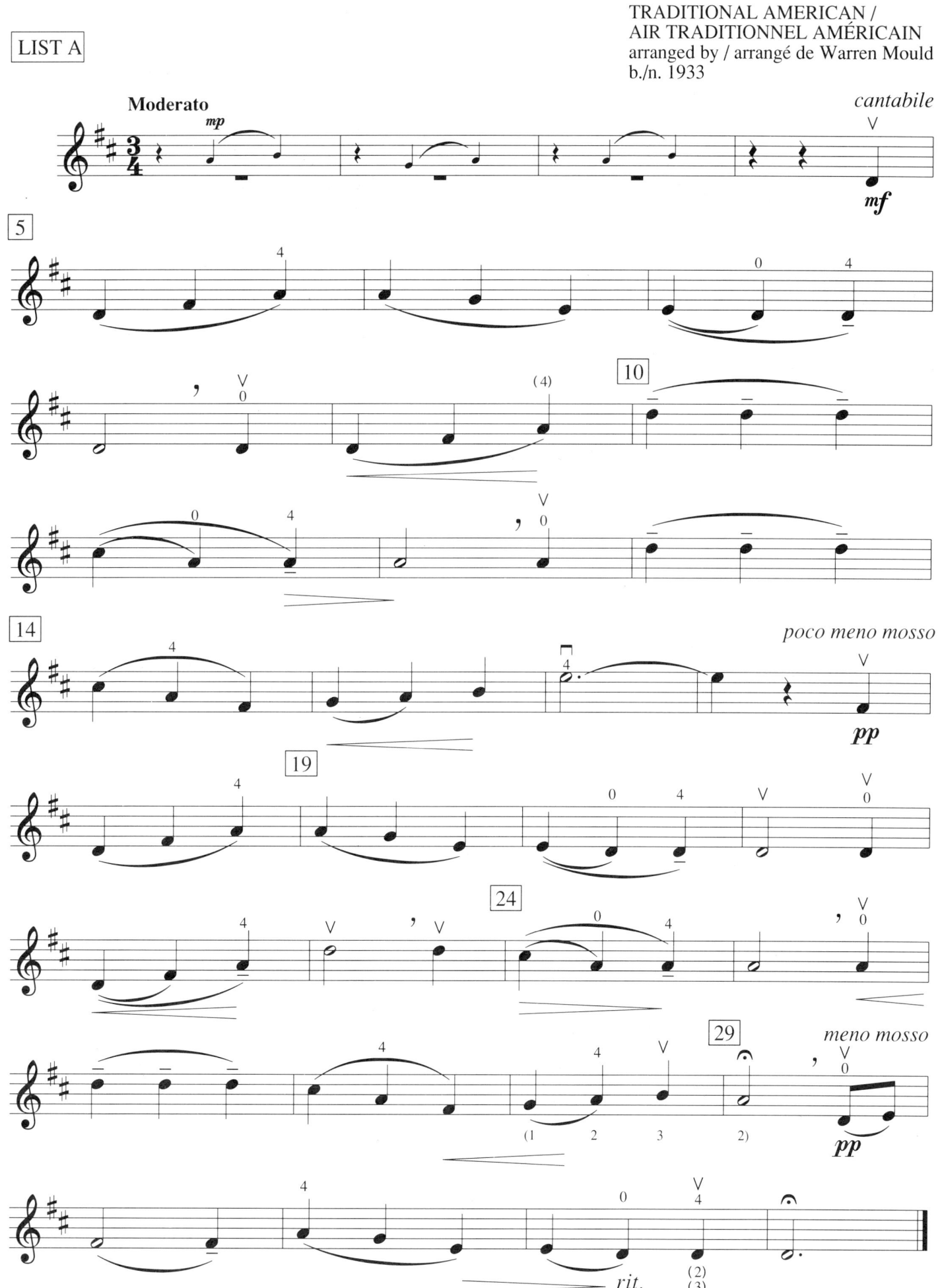

ANDANTE

LIST A

FRIEDRICH KUHLAU
1786-1832

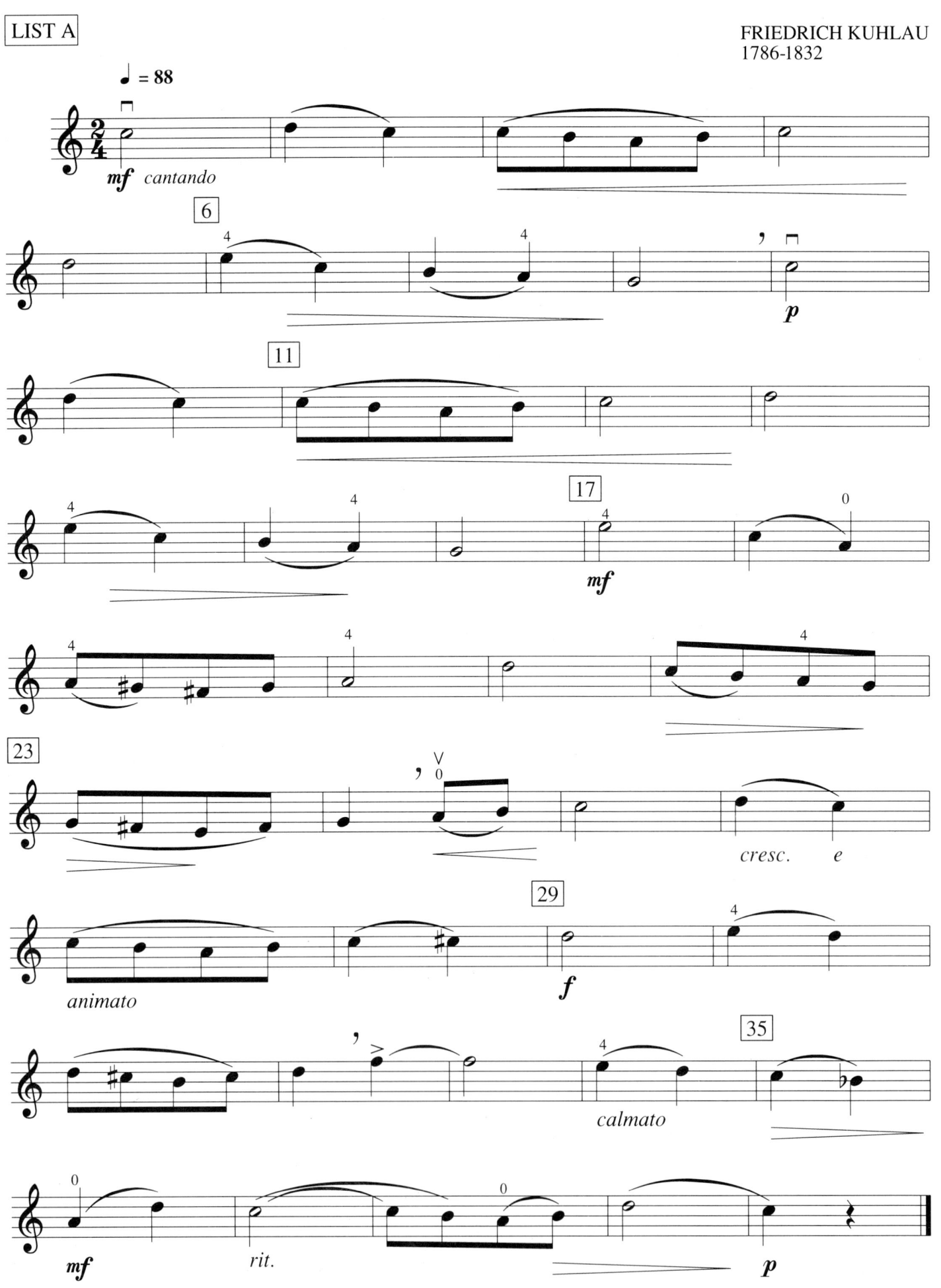

4

THE SAILBOAT ON THE LAKE / LE VOILIER SUR LE LAC

JEAN COULTHARD
b./n. 1908

LIST A

Floating gently /
Flottant doucement ♩ = 92

poco rit.

mp a tempo

poco rit.

mp a tempo cresc.

poco rit.

a tempo

gradually slower to the end /
en ralentissant jusqu' à la fin

mf poco rit. mp dim.

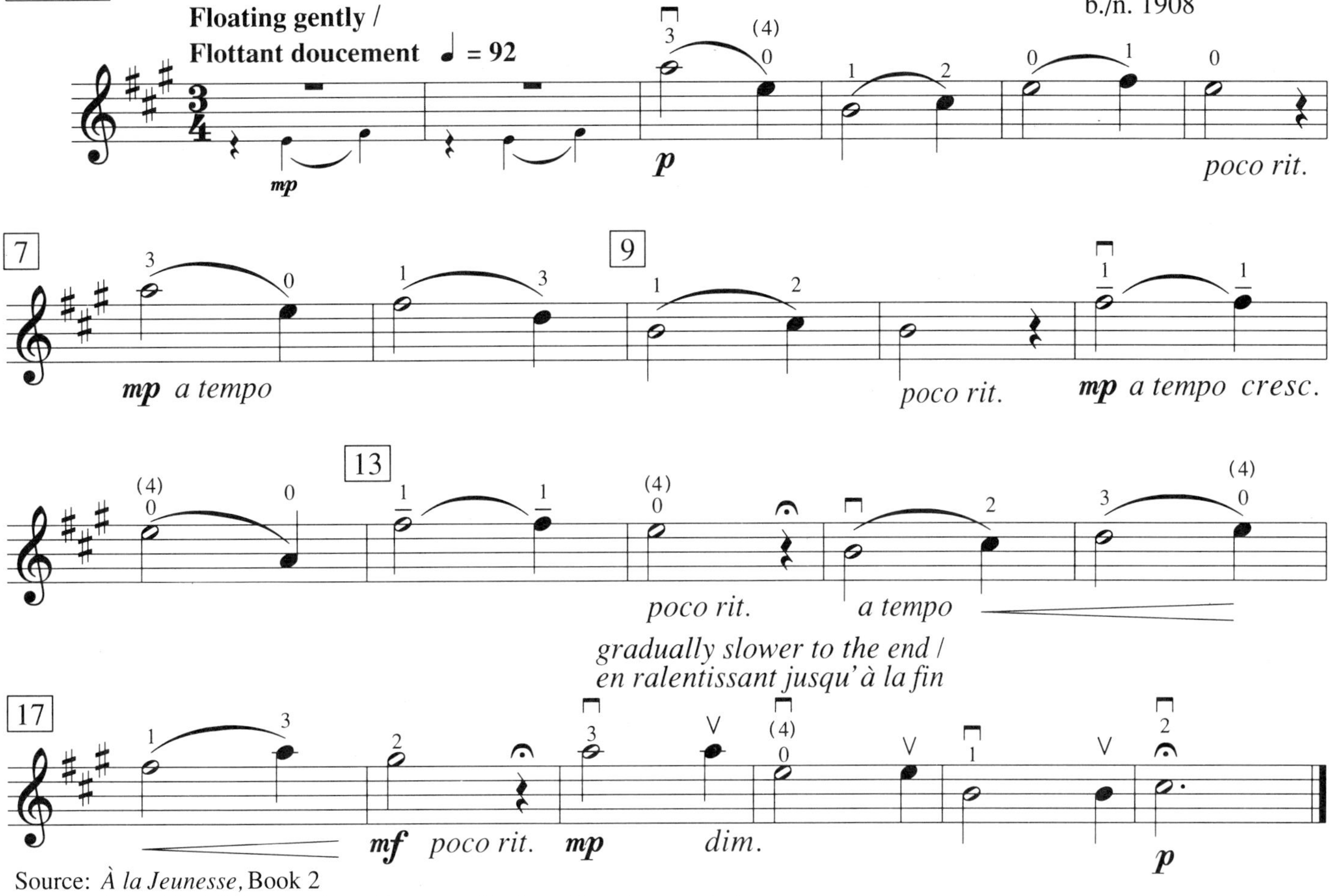

Source: *À la Jeunesse,* Book 2

MINUET / MENUET

CHRISTOPH WILLIBALD GLUCK
1714-1787

LIST A

Andante grazioso

cresc.

mf

Source: *"Que d'attraits,"* chorus from Act 1 of *Iphigénie en Aulide* (1744)

EVENING SONG / CHANSON DU SOIR

LIST A

GEORG C. SCHEMELLI
c. 1676-1762

The introduction is editorial. Use the enharmonic fingering indicated in measure 12. / L'introduction est de la part des rédacteurs. Utiliser le doigté enharmonique tel qu'est indiqué à la mesure 12.

Source: Schemelli's *Musicalisches Gesang-Buch,* no. 39 (1736), for which J.S. Bach supplied the figured bass. / *Musicalisches Gesang-Buch,* nº 39 (1736), de Schemelli, pour lequel J.S. Bach fournit la basse chiffrée.

Arrangement © copyright 1992 The Frederick Harris Music Co., Limited.

ON TIP-TOE / SUR LA POINTE DES PIEDS

LIST A

VIOLET ARCHER
b./n. 1913

Source: *Twelve Miniatures*
© Copyright 1982 Waterloo Music Company Limited. Used by permission.

THE WISH / LE VOEU

FRÉDÉRIC CHOPIN
1810-1849

Source: *Życzenie,* op. 74, no. 1 (1829)

FOLK SONG / CHANSON FOLKLORIQUE

TRADITIONAL HUNGARIAN /
AIR TRADITIONNEL HONGROIS
arranged by / arrangé de Hugh J. McLean
b./n. 1930

LIST A

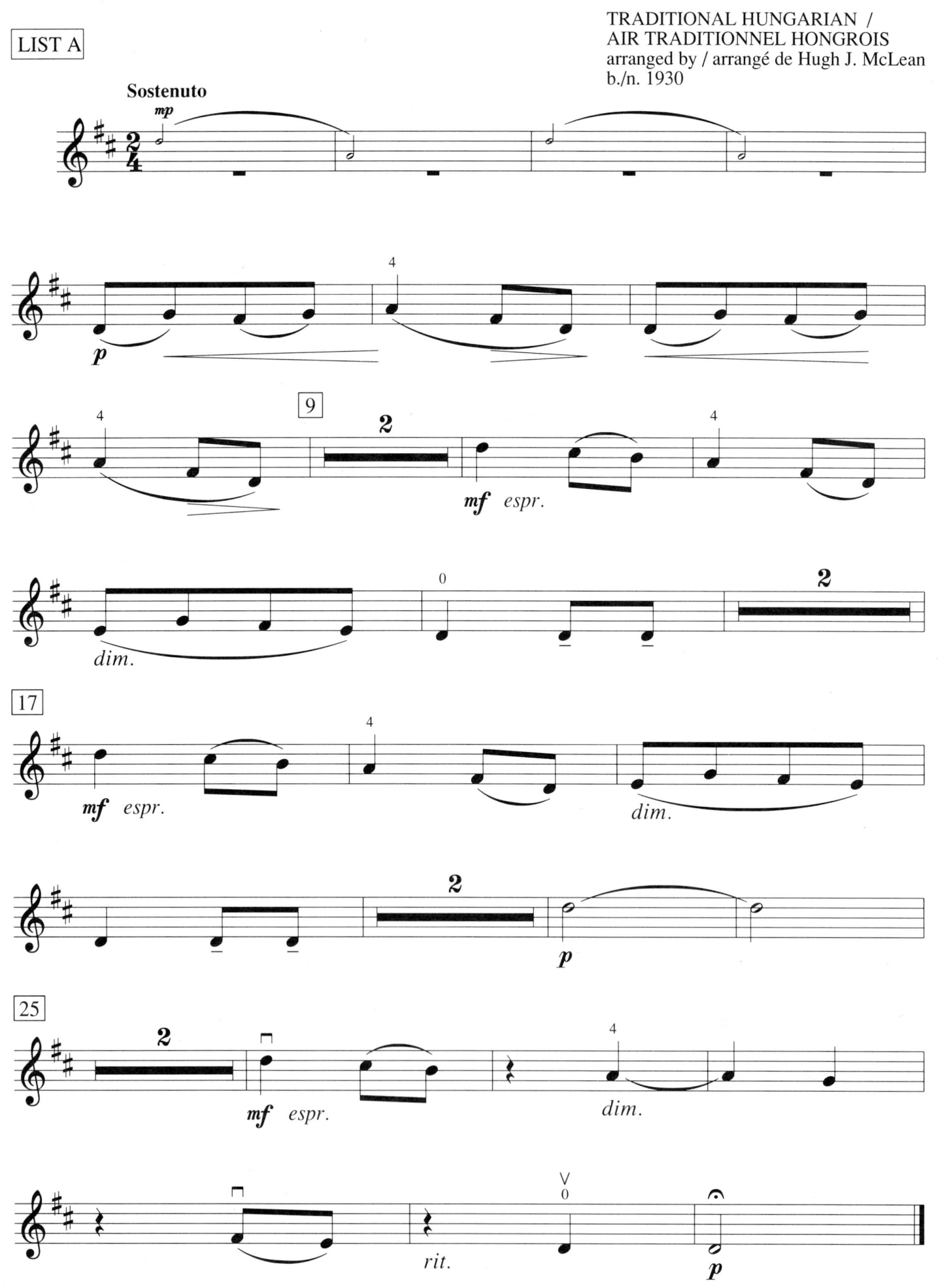

TURKISH MARCH / MARCHE TURQUE

LUDWIG VAN BEETHOVEN
1770-1827

LIST B

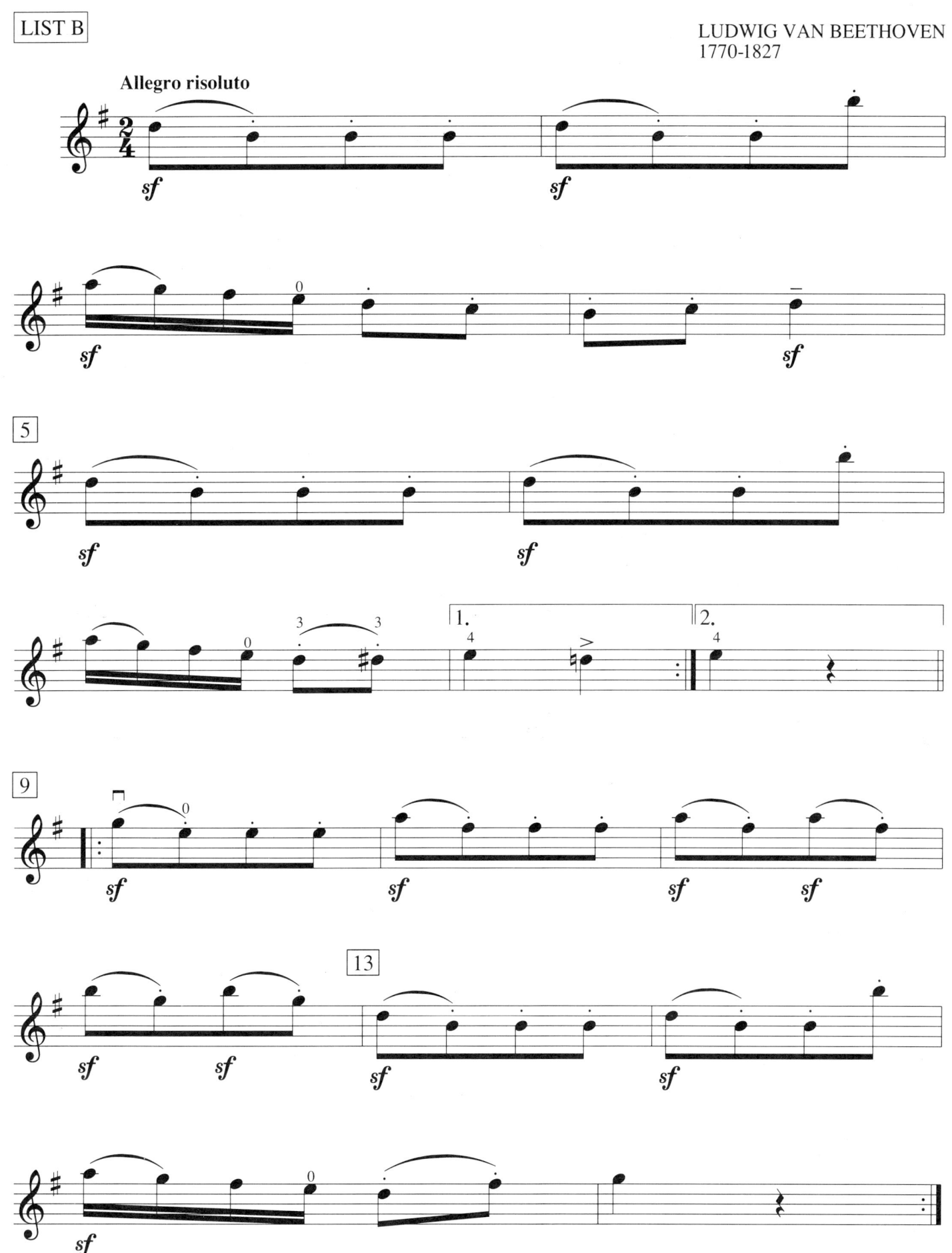

Source: *Six variations on an original theme,* op. 76 (1809)

BOURRÉE

LIST B

Allegro ♩ = 120-132

GEORGE FRIDERIC HANDEL
1685-1759

Source: *Water Music* (Suite in F, 1717)
Arrangement © copyright 1992 The Frederick Harris Music Co., Limited.

A LITTLE PIECE / UNE PETITE PIÈCE

LIST B

ROBERT SCHUMANN
1810-1856

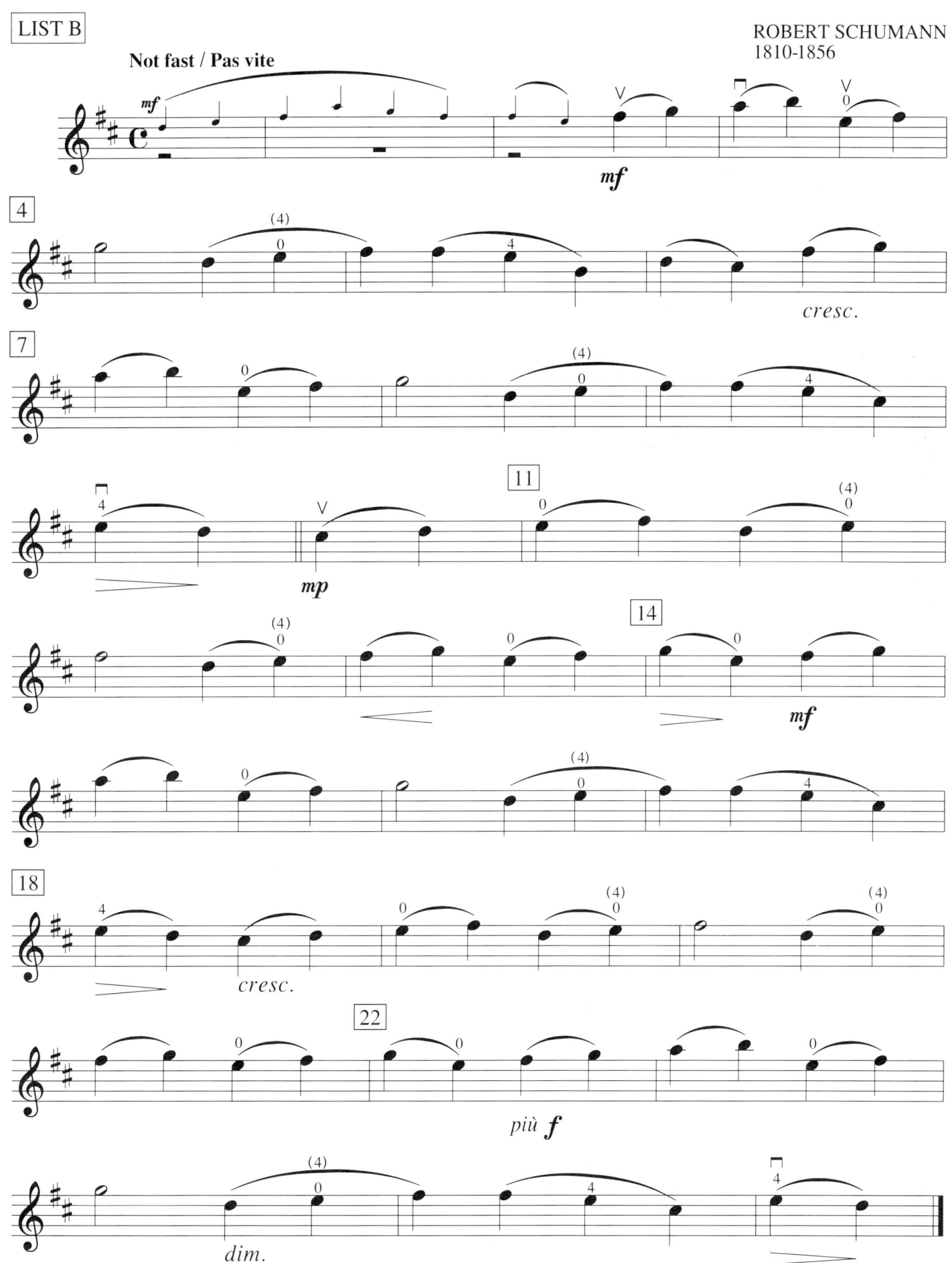

Source: *Album for the Young*, op. 68, no. 5 (1848)
Arrangement © copyright 1992 The Frederick Harris Music Co., Limited.

SONG AND DANCE / CHANSON ET DANSE

I

REZSÖ SUGÁR
b./n. 1919

SCOTTY LAD / LE P'TIT SCOTTY

LIST B

ROBERT FLEMING
1921-1976

**Martially (as fast as possible) /
Style martiale (aussi rapide que possible)**

MARCH / MARCHE

JEREMIAH CLARKE
c. 1674-1707

Arrangement © copyright 1992 The Frederick Harris Music Co., Limited.

HOMAGE TO BARTÓK / HOMMAGE À BARTÓK

JEAN ETHRIDGE
b./n. 1943

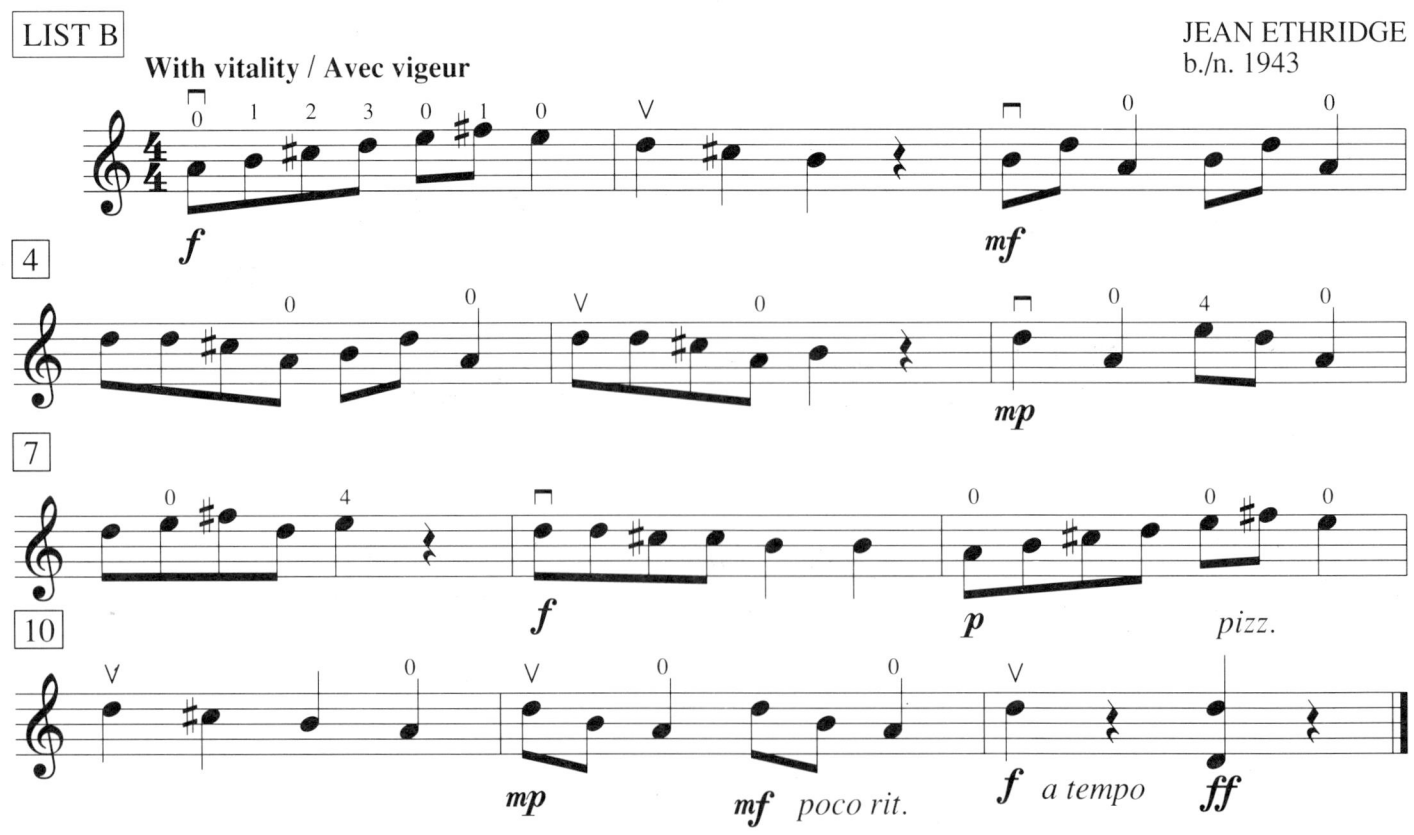

This piece is dedicated to Natalie Turner. / Cette pièce est dédiée à Natalie Turner.
Source: *Á la Jeunesse*, Book 1
© Copyright 1983 Waterloo Music Company Limited. Used by permission.

SOLDIER'S MARCH / MARCHE DU SOLDAT

LIST B

**Lively and in strict time /
Avec vivacité et en rythme strict** ♩ = 120

ROBERT SCHUMANN
1810-1856

Source: *Album for the Young*, op. 68, no. 2 (1848)
Arrangement © copyright 1992 The Frederick Harris Music Co., Limited.

THE GYPSY FIDDLER / LE VIOLONEUX TZIGANE

ELEANOR MURRAY
d./m. 1980

Composer's note: "When I play on my fiddle in Dooney / Folk dance like a wave of the sea. *W. B. Yeats*"

Source: *Tunes for My Violin*

© Copyright 1937 Hawkes & Son London Ltd. Used by permission of Boosey & Hawkes Music Publishers Limited.

LONGING FOR SPRING / EN SOUPIRANT APRÈS LE PRINTEMPS

WOLFGANG AMADEUS MOZART
1756-1791

Source: *Sehnsucht nach dem Frühlinge*, KV 596 (1791)

Arrangement © copyright 1992 The Frederick Harris Music Co., Limited.

THE WISH / LE VOEU

FRÉDÉRIC CHOPIN
1810-1849

LIST A

Source: *Życzenie*, op. 74, no. 1 (1829)

FOLK SONG / CHANSON FOLKLORIQUE

TRADITIONAL HUNGARIAN /
AIR TRADITIONNEL HONGROIS
arranged by / arrangé de Hugh J. McLean
b./n. 1930

LIST A

TURKISH MARCH / MARCHE TURQUE

LIST B

LUDWIG VAN BEETHOVEN
1770-1827

Source: *Six variations on an original theme*, op. 76 (1809)
Arrangement © copyright 1992 The Frederick Harris Music Co., Limited.

BOURRÉE

LIST B

GEORGE FRIDERIC HANDEL
1685-1759

Source: *Water Music* (Suite in F, 1717)

A LITTLE PIECE / UNE PETITE PIÈCE

LIST B

ROBERT SCHUMANN
1810-1856

Source: *Album for the Young*, op. 68, no. 5 (1848)

SONG AND DANCE / CHANSON ET DANSE

I

REZSÖ SUGÁR
b./n. 1919

N.B.: both pieces must be played in examination. / Les deux morceaux doivent être jouées pour l'examen.
© Copyright 1966 Editio Musica Budapest. Reprinted with kind permission of Editio Musica Budapest.

II

Allegretto

SCOTTY LAD / LE P'TIT SCOTTY

LIST B

ROBERT FLEMING
1921-1976

Martially (as fast as possible) /
Style martiale (aussi rapide que possible)

Ste. Anne's, Oct. 25/64

MARCH / MARCHE

LIST B

JEREMIAH CLARKE
c. 1674-1707

HOMAGE TO BARTÓK / HOMMAGE À BARTÓK

LIST B

JEAN ETHRIDGE
b./n. 1943

With vitality / Avec vigeur

This piece is dedicated to Natalie Turner. / Cette pièce est dédiée à Natalie Turner.

Source: *À la Jeunesse*, Book 1

SOLDIER'S MARCH / MARCHE DU SOLDAT

Source: *Album for the Young*, op. 68, no. 2 (1848)

THE GYPSY FIDDLER / LE VIOLONEUX TZIGANE

LIST B

ELEANOR MURRAY
d./m. 1980

Composer's note: "When I play on my fiddle in Dooney / Folk dance like a wave of the sea. *W.B. Yeats*"

Source: *Tunes for My Violin*

LONGING FOR SPRING /
EN SOUPIRANT APRÈS LE PRINTEMPS

WOLFGANG AMADEUS MOZART
1756-1791

Source: *Sehnsucht nach dem Frühlinge*, KV 596 (1791)

Arrangement © copyright 1992 The Frederick Harris Music Co., Limited.